I0437648

The Green Quest

Flossy Ifeyinwa Obuekwe, Ph.D.

authorHOUSE®

AuthorHouse™ UK Ltd.
500 Avebury Boulevard
Central Milton Keynes, MK9 2BE
www.authorhouse.co.uk
Phone: 08001974150

This book is a work of non-fiction. Unless otherwise noted, the
author and the publisher make no explicit guarantees as to the
accuracy of the information contained in this book and in some

First published by AuthorHouse 1/30/2009

ISBN: 978-1-4389-4225-4 (sc)

Printed in the United States of America
Bloomington, Indiana

This book is printed on acid-free paper.

Contents

Dedication

This Book has been Dedicated to All Children, Girls and Young Women who have died of HIV/AIDS Throughout The World,

I Love You All

Preface

This book has been written as a result of human trafficking and sex trade that have been very rampant amongst young girls and women in many parts of the world.

It has been also been written to encourage these young girls and women to see the consequences of getting involved in prostitution (**sex trade**). Even though many of them have come from very poor background, they should be encouraged to go to school, work and help their families.

They would need to get some education, become empowered and learn to say **"NO"** to **unsafe and unprotected sex**. They would also need to take some informed decisions on matters that concern them when they get **empowered.**

They should also get to know their **Reproductive Health Rights** when they become empowered. They would have to come to the terms of "**when, why,** and **how**" to get about their health rights and would no longer be intimidated because they are uneducated and poor.

Unfortunately, these are not happening, so, these young girls and women find themselves in extreme **"danger".**

These young girls and women should be taught to know that "unsafe and unprotected sex" can make them contract STDs and HIV and they could die of AIDS and leave behind their families, especially very children who would have nobody to care for them.

Don't be lured into prostitution girls!!!!!!!!

Empower Yourself!!!!!!!!!!!!!

Get some Education!!!!!!!!!!!!!

AIDS is real!!!!!!!!!!!

Protect yourself!!!!!!!!!!!!

It is indeed a global pandemic!!!!

Protect yourself!!!!!!!!!!!

Get some education and learn how to say **"No"** to **"unsafe and unprotected sex"**

Become independent!!!!!!!!!!!

Flossy I. Obuekwe

Author

Chapter One

Ijenma was only eight years old when she moved to the big city to live with her stepbrother, Emmanuel and his wife Rebecca. She had never been to school before and was to start the next school year which was just a couple of months away.

The young girl had never left her village Dagasto since she was born and had never seen or lived in a big city before. She and her mother were so excited when her stepbrother, Emmanuel drove down to the village in his car to pick her up for the long journey back to the big city.

Weeks before then, she had already told all her peers in the village about this great journey to the big city which she would be embarking on with her elder brother, Emmanuel. Most of her peers if any had never traveled out of the village too and to them this was a dream coming true for Ijenma. She had washed her clothes in the village stream, cut her hair and was ready to be picked up by her brother, Emmanuel. That evening, before all the young girls in her neighborhood came to bid her farewell in her father's compound, many of them were already crying and said they were going to miss her terribly. Some brought her gifts of fruits, yams, plantain, peanuts and palm oil as was traditional for someone either leaving or visiting their village. Her mother was very happy because she knew Ijenma would be opportune to go to school once she got to the big city and lived her step-brother, Emmanuel.

Ijenma was the first child from her own mother. She came from a polygamous family because her father had married two wives and her own mother was the younger of two. The evening before, her mother invited some of her mates from the village to a sumptuous dinner to tell them that her daughter was going to live in the big city with her elder brother. She was so excited as she served dinner that evening. Many people prayed for Ijenma and wished her well.

That morning before they left for the city, she had already packed all her clothes and shoes into a leather bag which her mother bought from the village market the previous day. Her step-brother Emmanuel would have to leave very early the next morning because the journey to the city would take them at least six hours on a very rough road. She sat at the back of the car, looking through the window and waving to her mother and other siblings who were up early to bid them goodbye.

A little drama ensued as they were leaving. Her mother burst into tears as well as her other siblings. Her father was embarrassed and asked why they were all crying instead of rejoicing that Ijenma was going to live in the big city. Her step-brother sensing the ugly situation, immediately drove off, leaving them standing there until the car disappeared before they went back into the house.

When her step-brother looked out through the car mirror, he noticed that, Ijenma was wiping out some tears from her eyes, apparently crying too, when she saw her mother and other siblings doing that. Her brother then yelled out at her and said:

"Ijenma, do you want to go back to the village or come and live with me in the big city?"

She never responded and they continued on their journey.

As it was getting to midday, they made a stop at a small local restaurant, half way between their journeys and had lunch together. Ijenma was so excited when the server brought her a plateful of rice, some pieces of meat and some juice and bottled water to go down with the food. She hurriedly ate up all the food, apparently very hungry, drank the juice and water that her brother had to ask if she wanted some more. She then said she was full and okay.

After a little rest, they continued on their journey to the big city. They finally got into the city three hours later and Ijenma was so amazed to see many cars going in opposite directions, something she never saw all through the time she lived in the village. She then started to ask her step-brother Emmanuel some curious questions.

"Brother Emmanuel, how come there are so many cars on these roads?

Can they not bump into each other the way they are moving very fast?"

Her step-brother laughed and replied:

"Ije, you will soon get used to seeing all these cars because they will fall within your daily life routine in the city."

She giggled. They finally arrived in her brother's home and out there to welcome them were her brother's wife and their three little children, **Somtor**, **Chikor** and **Ebukor**, aged seven, five and two respectively. They all went into the house together and the children were so excited to see Ijenma and asked her so many questions which she could not answer. Because the children could not speak their native language there was a communication gap between them and Ijenma. They could only speak English but she could not.

They all had supper together, had their evening bath because it was customary for them to do that so they could sleep well at night because of the hot weather.

Ijenma became part of her step-brother's family. When school resumed for the next school year, she was enrolled in grade one at the age of eight because she had never been to school before. She apparently was very dull and found it very difficult to read simple **a, b, c** .... alphabets, which her nephews and niece were already chanting off with. Well, it was pretty clear; she had never gone to school before and even if she did, was trying to adjust to her new environment. For some it could be trying to adjust to a new place while for others it could be very frustrating as well. She kept on moving and with her sister-in-law's help, managed to go through that year and was promoted to the next class. Her brother's wife was a high school teacher who spent extra hours with her, ensuring that she met up with her school work and assignments. That was very encouraging too for Ijenma.

She did very well at school and her step-brother and wife were very happy at her progress. She did all her home work and was always among the first ten students in any class she was in. Her step-brother was very proud of her. Ijenma visited the village for the first time three years after being in the big city. That day, she was like a "princess". People gathered from different compounds in her village to come and see her. Her mother and siblings were all dancing. Her father was very proud of his son, Emmanuel and thanked him for looking after her very well.

It was quite amazing because everyone said she had completely changed, looking very fresh and robust and had grown much taller. Her peers in the village were all admiring her. Her mother was so proud of her step-son and immediately started showering heavenly blessings on him. The most interesting part of this visit was that the very morning they were to go back to the big city, the family woke up to find two young girls of Ijenma's age group, whose mothers had sneaked into the compound in the early hours of the morning with their luggage. It was really a funny and sorry sight because their intention being that Emmanuel would also take them along to the big city too. This was not possible he told them and when they were leaving the children cried and ran after their car. It was really very sad to see that happen and everyone around felt very sorry for them.

The young girl continued with her life and education, still living with her step-brother, Emmanuel and his family in the big city. Instead of spending the normal six years in elementary school, Ijenma spent only five years because she appeared very smart and skipped a class. She passed the qualifying examination into secondary (high) school and finally got into junior secondary (high) school.

Her brother never wanted her to get into a trade or vocational school or even marry very early. He wanted Ijenma to become a nurse so that he would take her back to the village and brag about that great achievement. Ijenma appeared to be very bright as to offer science subjects and mathematics in senior secondary school. Incidentally, all over the school system in her country, mathematics and English subjects were compulsory for final senior secondary school certificate examination, so students could not run away from those subjects. She struggled on and did well with very good grades. Her brother was so happy and said that Ijenma never disappointed him. He wanted her to go to college but felt she could work for a year or two to get more mature and probably acquire some more skills.

Chapter Two

Ijenma finished high school and got her Senior School Certificate. Due to her step-brother's influence, she got a job as a Clerical Assistant with a Government Ministry in the big city where they lived. Her brother told her from the beginning that was just a temporary job, as he still wanted her to become a registered nurse but only wanted her to acquire some skills. Some of his children were ready to go to high school at this time. Ijenma worked for a few more years to gain some experience and better skills and Emmanuel insisted she must have some post-secondary education and this was where the trouble started with Ijenma.

She did not want to go back to school again having earned some little money. She felt very comfortable with what she earned at the time. Her brother told her that if she went to college, she would earn more and even become more independent.

At this time Ijenma was already over twenty-five years old and by the cultural norms of her society she was overdue for marriage. Meanwhile, she had started going out with this guy and when her brother's wife found out told her husband who never approved of that relationship. Ijenma said the young man had proposed to marry her but Emmanuel said that would never happen.

It was traditional for young girls from her culture to receive their family blessings before they went into any marriage contract. Emmanuel went home to complain to his father who already was getting very old that Ijenma was dating a man whom they have never approved of.

At this time, their father had been wondering why Ijenma had not yet seen a suitor in the city despite her good education. He thought to himself that, if she had remained in the village she would have been married off many years before. That disturbed him and Ijenma's mother so much that they expressed their disappointment and said those were the very reasons parents never allowed their young daughters to grow up in the big cities in their society. They decided to send her back to the village to teach her a good lesson, but that was even too late for Ijenma. This was a young girl who left her village many years ago to the big city. She went to elementary, junior and senior secondary (high) schools, worked for a couple of years and now being sent back home to the village to go and live.

Ijenma left her job in the city, came back to the village and lived there with her parents for almost two years. Life became very unbearable and also miserable for her. There was no electricity, no good roads and no good source of drinking water in their village. Every morning and evening she had to go down to the village stream which was about two kilometers away to fetch a bucket of water, which she carried on her head back to the house.

She must also bathe in the village stream before coming home because, there would not be enough water to use for household chores, let alone for bathing at home. This was too uncomfortable for Ijenma, especially when she had not lived in the village for over fifteen years or more at that time. She bore all the sufferings and still respected and obeyed her parents. Her father became more worried because suitors who came to ask for Ijenma's hand in marriage since she came back to live in the village from the big city were all rejected. She claimed they were not educated enough and so would not want anything to do with them. This made her father to become angrier.

One weekend, Emmanuel decided to come down to the village and asked Ijenma to get her things ready that she would be going back to the big city with him the following day. Ijenma was so excited to hear that. Since she came back to live in the village, suitors were coming from different clans to ask for her hand in marriage. Because she had grown up in the city, she looked down on these suitors as very inferior, with no education and would not even have enough money to keep her. This also made her father very angry and unhappy. Her step-brother, Emmanuel supported her and thought that at Ijenma's current level of exposure and education, it would be very difficult for her to marry a man from their village with little or no education. He then said that Ijenma should be considering suitors who were very educated; physicians, teachers, engineers, lawyers or accountants and never the peasant farmers from the village who had come asking for her hand in marriage.

What an irony of life!!!!!!!

This was a young girl who never tasted city life before and now scorned young men from the same village who came to propose to her.

Ijenma moved back to the city with her step-brother, Emmanuel and went back to work after two years of living with her parents in the village. When she got back to the city, life became so tough and rough for her. She was finding it very difficult to adjust and wondered within herself if office work was actually a good fit for her anymore. By then, trafficking in young girls and women was the order of the day and many young girls were '**sponsored**' abroad for prostitution ('**sex trade**'). Many of them were also lured into prostitution to other countries and their so-called "**sponsors**" initially told them and their parents that they had very good jobs out there waiting for them. Many of these young girls and women were also told there were many opportunities for them out there and they could earn '**hard currencies**' usually '**American Dollars**' by working in tomato farms or as "**nannies**" or '**caregivers**' and they could send money back home to their poor families. Very many of them accepted these offers and traveled abroad.

So many of these young girls **(fourteen years and older)** in the cities, dropped out from high schools and moved out for **"greener pastures"**

Very many found themselves in countries outside their fatherland. The fact was that many were too young and parents believed the 'sponsors'. This became acceptable and most parents as a result of being very poor had to borrow money from creditors and some even sold or used their family houses as collaterals. Many of them even pulled their daughters out from secondary schools and sent them **'abroad'** for **'greener pastures'.**

Most of these young girls and women never came back or paid up, so the creditors seized their parents' houses and drove entire families into the streets homeless. Some of these families became poorer than they were. Many who owned houses in the big cities had to go back to the village or live in rented accommodation because they had lost their family homes, some of which have been passed down through many generations as inheritance.

Some fathers of these young girls and women committed suicide because they lost all their life's savings to these agents. Despite these sad outcomes, some families were still borrowing money and selling off their properties to be able to send their daughters abroad for **'greener pastures'.** All warnings fell on deaf ears.

The question now is:

"What was the motive behind all these?"

One or two straight answers may follow:

Some of these young girls and women, who were able to find their way, got out there, did whatever they did, sent money back home, paid off their sponsors, bought cars for their parents and even built mansions for them.

For many of these families, their life styles automatically **"changed"**. A few others who saw what had taken place, fought hard to see that their own daughters followed the same pathway.

At the end, who lost out?

All of them did anyway!!!!!!!!!!!!!!!

Some of these young girls and women drowned and died as they were being ferried across the sea all in quest for **'greener pastures'**. No news of their deaths was ever sent home to their parents. As anyone would have imagined, not everyone was able to make it. Many of them died from heat and thirst.

"All in quest for greener pastures"

As they got there, many found out there was no job for them as promised by their 'sponsors', so they went into prostitution as a last resort. Many fell into the hands of the law enforcement of the host countries and were arrested and sent to prison. Those who became involved in 'sex' trade were immediately deported. When not deported, they were thrown into jails and family members never got to know this sad part of the story, while "sponsors" kept saying they arrived safely and were doing well. This usually was the beginning of their nightmares.

Many of these young girls and women went through these horrifying ordeals and those that finally managed to come home told their horrifying stories. Yet, parents kept selling off their inherited family homes to send out their daughters for **'greener pastures'**.

Some told stories of how they were usually left in the streets at nights and asked to follow any **'John'** who came around. They were usually picked off the streets in the early hours of the mornings by their so-called 'sponsors'. This was really awful and scary to hear.

These stories were told by every group deported home and yet they fell on deaf ears. Parents and especially mothers kept selling off all they had and even borrowed money from creditors to send out their young daughters to get involved in these dehumanized "trades".

Governments, religious, community and women leaders became concerned about these dehumanized acts especially encouraged by mothers and families themselves. Parents were threatened to be sent to jail if their daughters were involved in these dehumanizing acts and these threats still fell on deaf ears.

Chapter Three

One evening as Emmanuel returned home from work, he found a note addressed to him lying at the centre table in his living room. He knew immediately that was his sister, Ijenma's hand writing. Panicking and with shaky hands he opened and read it. He suddenly slumped into a sofa and shouted:

"Oh my God, you mean this girl finally joined this bad group?!!!! Where did she get the money for the trip from?!!!!!!!

What would I tell my old father in the village?"

He started sweating profusely and began to cry. His wife ran out of the room and enquired to know what was actually going on. He just gave her the letter to read. She never expressed any surprise at Ijenma's behavior but only said:

"I had always seen the hand writing on the wall and knew that was coming very fast.

Are you surprised Emmanuel?"

- She asked her husband.

Ijenma had left that morning for **"greener pastures"** according to her note. She said she borrowed money from a creditor using their father's house in the village as collateral. She said she hoped to pay back the money within one year because she would try to work very hard as soon as she arrived.

Emmanuel was still under shock for the next couple of hours. He could not believe that the little girl he picked up from the village some years back had now turned into

....

"I can't believe this, wonders shall never end," he said.

That evening he refused to eat his dinner and was so sad and very disappointed despite much persuasion from the wife. He did not sleep well either because he kept tossing on the bed all night. Anyway, he made up his mind to get back to the village as quickly as he could to inform his father and step-mother on the real situation of things. He was really very nervous and scared on how to break the news to his father because his old man's health had deteriorated so much in the past one year and feared that could aggravate a heart attack for him. He then decided to go home first and meet with his uncles, whom he believed would be in a better position to give some advice.

He decided to go and meet with his church pastor in the city. He scheduled a meeting with him the following day. When they met, he showed him Ijenma's letter. His pastor was surprised to read that Ijenma had gone according to her **"for greener pastures".** It was also shocking to him because he had known Ijenma since he came from the village to live with her brother Emmanuel and had seen her grown from a young girl into a woman.

He too was in shock and asked Emmanuel to go back to the village and intimate his family members about the situation. Emmanuel himself was confused and regretted having ever brought his sister Ijenma to live with him in the city.

The following day he set out on his journey to the village. When he got there, his father was sitting out on the balcony with some guests. He rushed out to meet Emmanuel at the car as was his usual practice. There and then he read his countenance and asked if all was well. Emmanuel told him he was only tired from the long journey from the city to the village. His step-mother was not home but his other siblings prepared dinner for him. He had his bath and while he was having dinner, his step-mother came in and was so surprised to see him at home. She asked of every family member in the big city including Ijenma and he told her everyone was fine. That evening, he told his father he wanted to go and see his uncle, whom he said he had never seen for a while. His father wanted to come along with him but he said it would not be all that necessary because he wanted to be brief with the visit at his uncle's.

A few yards away from his uncle's house, Emmanuel heard his voice and in the usual traditional way and using his titled name, Emmanuel greeted him:

"Nnabueze (Father is King), I greet you", he said.

The old man on hearing Emmanuel's voice responded immediately: ***"Emma,*** *my son, where are you coming from this night?*

I hope all is well my son?"

Emmanuel retorted by saying:

"That is why I am here tonight, Nnabueze".

He helped his uncle bring out some chairs out on the balcony where they sat while Emmanuel told him the whole story about Ijenma's trip for **'greener pastures'**. How she had used their father's house in the village for collateral in borrowing money from her sponsors, which she hoped to pay back within one year. The old man was just taken aback and shouted:

"Children of these days think they are much wiser than those of my ancestors!!!!!!!!!!!!!!

Imagine a small girl like Ijenma using her family house here in the village as collateral to borrow money to travel abroad for prostitution!!!!!!!!!!!!!!!!!!!!

Wonders shall never end!!!!!

May the God my ancestors never avenge this!!!!!!!!"

Emmanuel then started to cry and wondered what could become of their old father, especially if his sister Ijenma could not repay the loan and her "sponsors" fought back and took away their family house. His uncle decided that they should never mention the situation yet to any family member until the condition became very bad.

Emmanuel finally went back to his father's compound to stay the night.

The following day he left for the city and as he was just driving into his house in the city, his cell phone rang and behold, there was Ijenma on the line. She started to cry and apologized for the stress her brother must be going through as a result of what she had done and not telling them of her initial plans before taking off for **'greener pastures'**. She wanted to let him know she arrived safely and would start working in a couple of days.

Emmanuel then asked her:

"Ijenma, what are you doing in whatever country you are calling from?

What type of work have you already found?

I hope you are not involved in 'sex' trade?"

As soon as she heard that Ijenma hung up the phone and never called back again.

Emmanuel became more worried and decided to play the man he was and never thought o Ijenma again. He said   to himself:

"ijenma is a grown woman, why am I tearing myself apart for her sake? I have my own life to live and my children are there for me too"

Chapter Four

As the years rolled by, no one ever heard anything about Ijenma again. She decided to cut everyone off and never called home again. She never called or wrote her step-brother Emmanuel who became very worried, especially when their parents kept asking about her. Life continued to become very difficult for Emmanuel. He had to take care of his immediate family (wife and three children) and his extended family in the village (parents, and three other siblings).

It was not really quite easy for him to do that, yet he managed and did his best. It was customary in their culture that having helped out in Ijenma's education, she in turn would help train other members of the family. This sort of became a chain reaction in an extended family system in their culture. But with Ijenma not being there to help, it was actually becoming very tough for Emmanuel to handle all these alone.

He bore it alone and also like a man. He did not want his sister's absence to bother him, but kept thinking what he was going to tell his parents in case the 'inevitable' happens. He was really very scared to the bones and did not know what to do or say. Occasionally, he would hear from his uncle in the village who would call to know what the situation was. Life started to be rough and tough for Emmanuel. He had to send food and provisions to his parents in the village, pay tuition for his three other siblings and look after his own three children.

Even though his wife was by him, he felt he was not doing enough or his immediate family. He continued to struggle on hoping that one day his circumstance would improve and asked for prayers from his church.

One evening as he drove in from work after almost a year or more since Ijenma left for **'greener pastures'**, and entered his living room, a young lady named **Cabrina** was seated on the sofa waiting for him. He asked whob she was and she said she was a friend of Ijenma and that they both lived together abroad. She was visiting her family and so Ijenma gave her a letter for her step-brother, Emmanuel. She said Ijenma instructed that the letter should never be given to anyone else except Emmanuel himself, and that was why she had waited for so long to hand over the letter personally to him. He asked if all was well with Ijenma and if she was still alive. The young lady laughed out so hilariously that Emmanuel was very embarrassed.

He carefully opened the letter, read through the contents. Ijenma left a phone number where she could be reached and asked Emmanuel to call her immediately he received her letter. He was so nervous and uncomfortable and did not actually know what was going on. Right there in front of the young lady, he called Ijenma and she responded immediately.

He relaxed as soon as he heard her voice and spoke to her again for the first time in almost a year. She said it had been very tough and rough for her and she never expected life was going to be that rough. She then told her step-brother she was working in a tomato farm during the day and in a restaurant at night as a waitress.

Emmanuel caught in immediately and asked:

"Ijenma, doing what at the restaurant in the night"

After they finally talked at length, Ijenma told her brother Emmanuel that there was a bank cheque for him with the visitor, Cabrina, which should be cashed immediately. She then handed him a cheque for five thousand (USD) United States Dollars. When Emmanuel received the cheque, he almost slumped into the chair because he had never seen that amount of money in his life before. He asked Cabrina what his sister Ijenma was actually doing there to be able to send him that amount of money.

Cabrina told him Ijenma had been working very hard to ensure that her sponsors were paid back and especially when she had used their father's house in the village as collateral for her trip. She then asked her brother to convert the money into the local currency, pay off her sponsors and whatever was left should be used to buy some provisions (groceries) and send to their parents in the village.

Emmanuel heaved a sigh of relief, thanked his guest and offered her some drinks. She declined and said she was very much in a hurry and had some other families whose daughters lived with them abroad to visit and deliver some packages. That night, Emmanuel started having a second thought about his sister's trip overseas.

He said to himself:

"If Ijenma was telling the truth about what she was actually doing there, then she could save our family from poverty"

He went to the bank, converted the money into the local currency, paid off his sister's sponsors, sent some money and provisions (groceries) to their parents in the village as

Ijenma had requested. It was during this trip that he finally told their parents that Ijenma had been out of the country for over a year and that she had sent some money and asked him to bring in the provisions to them. Ijenma's mother was so happy to hear that and their father then asked:

"When is she coming back home to get married Emmanuel?

Her mates are all married here with two or more children.

By our tradition, she is getting very old and no man would want to marry an old lady here in this village"

Emmanuel was silent. At this time Ijenma was already twenty-seven years old and all her peers in the village had married many years before and had two or more children.

Even her younger sister Onyins was already married with a child. This gave her father a lot of concern and he was very worried for Ijenma. Six months later, Ijenma sent home more money to her brother Emmanuel, instructing him to ensure that a very descent building was constructed in their family compound. A house that would be befitting to a man whose daughter was living abroad. He obeyed all her instructions to the letter and built a big mansion that was actually "befitting" to a man whose daughter was living abroad and sending money back home regularly.

Her mother was very happy but her father wanted her to come back home and get married because, according to him, she was already getting very old and her peers in the village were all married.

Tongues started wagging in the village about her family new lifestyle because the family status had suddenly changed. She opened a supermarket (grocery store) for her mother in front of their family compound in the village. She also bought her new clothes (wrappers) and some jewelleries and asked her to be always well-dressed at all times to depict a mother whose daughter lived abroad and regularly sent in money for her parents' up-keep. She then bought a car for her parents and hired a driver because according to her, they were too old to drive. Ijenma started making serious arrangements to see if her youngest sister, Nkosi would come over and live with her abroad. Brother

Emmanuel hesitated initially as he was still the family's spokesman, but after much pressure from family members, he gave in and allowed Nkosi to join Ijenma.

Ijenma made all adequate arrangements for her sister to come over. She bought the flight tickets, arranged for her visa and Nkosi finally joined her abroad. They lived together and it was only then that a family member was able to know that Ijenma was involved in 'sex' trade. Ijenma continued to send money home to their parents and their life style really changed. Barely a year after Nkosi came to join her sister Ijenma, tragedy struck and their old father passed away. This came as a very big blow to Ijenma and her sister Nkosi as well as their step-brother, Emmanuel. They all started making arrangements for their father's burial immediately.

Emmanuel already had enough load on him and had been wondering how he was going to cope with the costs of his father's burial. Being the first son of his father and as a full-grown adult, it was customary for him to foot the costs of his father's burial but he was not rich enough to carry on alone. He did not know where to start from. Ijenma called him and asked to know what he thought their father's burial could cost the family. Emmanuel heaved a sigh of relief when he realized that help was coming from his step-sister, Ijenma. He sent out the list to Ijenma who said she would bear all the costs of their father's funeral.

For the first time since Ijenma left for **'greener pastures'**, she came home during her father's burial. She covered all the expenses incurred for the burial and anyone would think she was the first son of the late man by tradition. Emmanuel was very uncomfortable because it was obvious to all that attended the funeral rites that it was Ijenma who paid for all the costs incurred during their father's burial. She lavished money. She brought in different dance groups and people had so much to eat and drink. She really spent money and her uncles were all impressed. One of them sarcastically said he wished ijenma was a man. No one in the village cared to ask what Ijenma was doing abroad where she lived, to be able to spend that amount of money for her father's burial.

All they knew was that her father had been given a 'befitting' burial. She squandered and lavished money and was praised by the village dancers as she was throwing money on them while they danced. It was really very disgusting.

All through the four weeks Ijenma spent in the village for her father's burial, she was beseeched at home by parents of young girls in their village who wanted her to take along their daughters back with her from wherever she came from. According to some of them, they were very impressed with her for being able to bury her father single-handedly. It was quite unbelievable the number of visitors in their home because at times her mother would have to tell some lie that she was not home. Some mothers were actually crying when she told them it was not possible to go back with their daughters at that time.

They never cared about what she was doing there and the kind of life Ijenma was living out there. All they wanted was to make sure their daughters left for **'greener pastures'** so they too could come out of poverty like Ijenma's family had done.

Very ridiculous, isn't it? Quite ridiculous indeed!!!!!!!!

Ijenma gave her father a **'befitting burial'** according to her village traditions and custom. She slaughtered ten cows, brought in traditional dancers from all walks of life and fed the whole village for two weeks. This was quite amazing and people were thrilled. This was what really attracted other mothers from their village who desperately wanted her to go back with their daughters. They never cared what the girls would go out there and do. All they wanted was for the young girls to bring back 'goodies' to them and never cared what they were going to do, even when they could lose their precious lives.

Before Ijenma finally left, she promised that she would ensure that at least five of the young girls would join her within the next one month or two and she really kept to her promise. Whatever way this was done, Ijenma was able to **'sponsor'** the five girls just as she promised, and they all joined her abroad to live with her and her younger sister Nkosi.

Whatever it was they did there, within the next three months these girls also started remitting money back home to their own parents. That was all everyone wanted to see or hear about. The story went round again and everyday Ijenma's mother would have tens of desperate mothers waiting at her gate and pleading that Ijenma should make adequate arrangements to take their own daughters abroad too. Ijenma became a great **'sponsor'** and a **"superstar"** in her village. Her family was respected as a result of this and her mother regarded with high esteem by other women in the village. She was not taking money from very close family members back home to bring their daughters abroad. She felt most of them were too poor to raise money for their daughters' trips. All she did was that those girls who were very close to her paid her directly as soon as they started making their own money abroad.

Everyone thought she was very generous and kind to have done that. For others, their families must have to fund their trips or they would not go.

Many of these families sold their farm lands, family houses, in fact all that they owned to be able to fund these trips for their daughters. Some even went as far as borrowing money from creditors with the hope they would repay them as soon as their daughters started sending money back home. For very many of them, this backfired and the creditors seized their family homes and they became homeless. Some of them turned into fugitives overnight. Out of greed, many families lost their homes and became **'beggars'** and **'squatters'** overnight.

Chapter Five

As years rolled by, Ijenma still remained unmarried and this bothered her mother and step-brother, Emmanuel. No young man from their village would even come closer because they thought people would say they were asking for her hand in marriage because she was rich. This actually bothered her mother because in their culture a woman who was not married was regarded as very unsuccessful, an outcast and worthless, even if she owned the whole world. Her step-brother, Emmanuel was also concerned about her situation too and had no control over that anyway.

Many years after Ijenma had gone back abroad after coming home for her father's burial, it dawned on her that by tradition their family house and the compound within its enclave belonged to her brother Emmanuel who was her father's first son and just her step-brother. Definitely she must have been advised by her mother and maternal relatives when she came home for her father's burial, because in the near future her own full-blood brothers would have grown into full adults and would have to leave the compound for Emmanuel as was the tradition and custom of their land, unless they were very poor themselves and have no place to go to. As a result of this societal norm, she decided to buy another plot of land very close to her family compound in the village to build another big house, this time for her mother and siblings.

Emmanuel was not happy about this and became very jealous of his step-sister, Ijenma, but friends and other family members told him that he should be very thankful to God and count himself as very lucky that Ijenma had already taken over his responsibilities by building a 'big' house in their family compound and also given their late father a 'befitting' burial. Ijenma continued to 'thrive' in her 'sex' trade and kept sending money home for very large projects. She sent her younger brothers to college and made sure her mother was very comfortable too.

Her sister Nkosi was not very comfortable with the 'sex' trade business and threatened to tell their step-brother, Emmanuel if

Ijenma did not let her off the hook. They started having some conflict and Nkosi then moved out of the house and rented her own apartment. They stopped talking and seeing each other and Nkosi vowed never to visit her again, unless she abandoned her shameful profession. All these fell on deaf ears and Ijenma continued with her life.

As time went on, Ijenma's health appeared to be deteriorating. Later on, she became very ill and Nkosi appeared very worried about this even though they have not been seeing or talking to each other for a while. She urged Nkosi never to tell or let anyone back home know that she was sick.

Nkosi became very confused and uncomfortable as Ijenma's condition became worse. A couple of months later, she wrote to their step-brother Emmanuel saying that Ijenma had been very sick, always appeared tired and could not even go about her daily routine and that she (Nkosi), was beginning to get worried for her.

Everyone in the family was also beginning to get worried for Ijenma as well. They did not know what was actually wrong with her and her step-brother then asked her to come back home. Instead of her mother condemning her nefarious activities, she said the **'village witches'** were hunting her daughter because she was doing very well in her business and they were all jealous of her success. What a statement to be made by a mother whose daughter had been involved in prostitution abroad.

Ijenma was asked to come back home as her condition got worse. She had been in bed for many months at that time and had lost a lot of weight. She never wanted to go and see a physician again. She refused to eat, appeared very pale and malnourished. She could not eat anything and her condition was getting worse and this put a lot of fears in her sister, Nkosi who did not know the next step to take. She again called their senior brother Emmanuel who now spoke with Ijenma, but she could not talk much because she was very weak and always appeared tired. It appeared she was hiding so many things from people, even from her younger sister, Nkosi.

About a year earlier, Ijenma had been diagnosed as having AIDS, but she never told anyone, even her own full-blood sister, Nkosi. She knew she was dying and also that she never lived a decent, safe, responsible and protective life. She was actively involved in prostitution (sex trade) while she told her family members she was working in a tomato farm and a restaurant. She had had **'unprotected sex'** all though her life for the sake of money. At the time she was at the prime of her youth, she sold her body for money which she sent home to her family who never asked or cared about what she did or where the money was coming from.

She made her family to live a descent and comfortable life in their community, lived in a big house, and had basically everything they wanted from this young lady. Now she was dying as a result of her promiscuous life and there was no family member around to come to her rescue. She was all alone in a strange land with her younger sister, Nkosi whom she never told what was going on in her life.

She struggled and struggled with life and still refused to see any physician, never took her medications because she felt she was going to die and always counted herself as a **'total failure'**.

Despite all the money she made by changing the lifestyle of her family members and relations, Ijenma was never happy at this last stage of her life. Every now and then, her sister Nkosi would hear her heave a sigh of relief, saying to herself, how terrible a life she had lived.

One fateful morning after having gone through the stresses of the condition she put herself in, Ijenma passed on to the great beyond. This was a young girl who had been full of life, hopeful, empowered, ambitious and had a very bright future, spent all her life in prostitution, looking for money, made the money, had unsafe and unprotected sex and finally contracted HIV and came down with AIDS. Ijenma's life was shattered. It was too late for her. She thought she made whatever money that was out there to make through prostitution (sex trade) to change her family's lifestyle, but she never lived to enjoy her life. She did not enjoy the fruits of her so-called labor, because she had labored in vain.

She ruined her life, herself, trying to live an indecent life. At this time can we say that Ijenma was a very greedy girl? We should not be judgmental, anyone would say!!!!!!!!!!!!!!

Her sister Nkosi was very terrified. She was all alone in a strange land without any family member out there. At this time she needed someone around to comfort her. She kept on saying to herself:

'What have I come out here to do?

I would have been married back home and probably had my own children!!!!

Why am I really here?'

Look at me in such a big mess, all in quest for greener pastures!!!!!!!!

Nkosi kept on lamenting and was taking instructions on the phone from her step-brother, Emmanuel on every next step to be taken towards bringing Ijenma's remains back home.

Poor girl, she cried her eyes out. Arrangements were already in place to bring Ijenma's remains back home to the village. Nkosi was also shattered because it was only when she came abroad to live with her sister Ijenma that she knew her sister was involved in a horrifying 'sex' trade.

For days, she noticed Ijenma would not come home and when she did, she would bring in plenty of money. One day she summoned up enough courage to ask Ijenma where she normally got all the money she brought home from. Ijenma snapped back and told her she should be happy and thankful that she brought her out for **'greener pastures'** because she would have been languishing in poverty back home. Nkosi felt very bad about her sister's statement and never asked her questions again when she came home late at night after that, until she left and rented her own apartment.

Emmanuel was wondering what he was going to tell his kinsmen and women when Ijenma's remains would be flown back home. He too was confused and shattered because their tradition and custom demanded that the casket must be opened for all their kinsmen and women to see if it was actually the remains of their daughter Ijenma that had been brought home for burial. At this very time that she died, Ijenma's body looked like a "skeleton" for she had emaciated so much that no one would even recognize her. She died of AIDS and people at home already knew what it was and looked like for anyone to die of AIDS in their community. Ijenma's remains was finally brought home accompanied by all the young girls she **'sponsored'** to join her abroad after her father's burial and her own younger sister, Nkosi.

They all cried their eyes out on their flight back home because she was supposed to be their **'mentor'**, **"role model"** and **'sponsor'** in prostitution.

Whatever it was she taught them could never be anything but how to succeed in prostitution (sex trade).

Her family tried to cover up by saying she was kidnapped and tortured because she was rich, instead of telling the truth. News had already spread round the village that she died of AIDS despite the cover up by her immediate family members. Her mother was devastated as well as her other siblings when Nkosi finally told them the true story. They were all told to keep their mouth shut so that neighbors and other family members would not know what actually went wrong with Ijenma. Even though Ijenma's family tried to give her a 'befitting' burial because she had the resources, it did not make sense.

Of what use was Ijenma's life after all?

We need not be judgmental at this point again anyway!!!!!!!

Ijenma was a very young woman bubbling with life, full of energy, ambitious, empowered and had lots of potentials. She had always wanted to further her education and be able to live an independent and comfortable life. Unfortunately, she became carried away by the greed and fast life in her society at that time, as well as peer-group influence and tried to reap where she had not sown. She got herself involved in prostitution, had unprotected sex, 'made quick money' and finally contracted HIV and died of AIDS.

She came around but never succeeded or conquered. After Ijenma's burial, her sister Nkosi refused to go back as well as some of the other girls who came back with them. No suitor had ever asked for the hands of any of those girls in marriage since they came back from abroad because people had been afraid of contracting HIV not to talk of dying of AIDS, especially from young girls and women who had gone abroad for **'greener pastures'**.

Chapter Six

This story has been written as an eye opener to young girls and women all across the world and especially in developing countries who are lured into human trafficking and prostitution ('sex' trade). They are usually deceived into believing that they are going to work as **'nannies'**, **'caregivers'** or in tomato farms, fast-food restaurants and grocery stores where they can make enough money to send back home to their poor families. This statement may never be true for so many. They should be very much aware that they can be tricked and lured into prostitution or even 'human trafficking'. Any young girl, who has not finished secondary (high) school, definitely will have no qualifications to find any descent job out there. They are only being deceived.

To be forewarned is to be fore-armed!!!!!!!!!!!!!!!
Be warned!!!!!!!!!!!!
Don't fall into their trap!!!!!!!!!

Getting involved in prostitution (sex trade), especially unsafe and unprotected sex at any age can cause you your life.

You may contract HIV, die of AIDS and spread it to other innocent people in the community.

Don't be lured into prostitution, Girls!!!!!!!!!!!!

Empower Yourself!!!!!!!!!!!!

Get Educated!!!!!!!!!!!!!!!

AIDS is real and presently has no cure!!!!!!!!!!

Protect Yourself!!!!!!!!!!!!

Millions of innocent people (children, youth and adults) have died of AIDS world wide. Millions of children have been orphaned as a result of their parents dying of AIDS

AIDS is indeed a global pandemic!!!!!!!!

Protect yourself!!!!!!!!!!!!

Empower yourself!!!!!!!!!!!!!!!

Get more **EDUCATION** and become

Independent!!!!!!!!!!!!

Author:

Flossy I. Obuekwe

www.ingramcontent.com/pod-product-compliance
Lightning Source LLC
Chambersburg PA
CBHW031301280526
45784CB00004B/1945